*It's your*

# FUTURE

## 25 RULES
### FOR SUCCESS IN AND OUT
### OF THE CLASSROOM

By Andre J. Benjamin

It's Your Future

Cover Designed by Key Jude
Interior design by Perseus Design

ISBN-13: 978-1482388992
ISBN-10: 1482388995

# IT'S YOUR FUTURE

"It's Your Future" is a tour that I conduct around the nation. The tour emphasizes the precious gift of today that each one of us have. Youth around the nation are dying and getting into trouble at an alarming rate. Given the troubling state of youth, I decided to take my life experience and challenge youth to look at themselves and make better decisions.

I wrote this rulebook as a guide for each young person facing tough decisions daily. In my own life I have made a lot of mistakes. I have also made some great decisions that produced great consequences. What you are about to read are rules that I know will make a great impact on your life's success. These rules are based on my own personal experiences as well as things that I have learned from people much older than me — people who have been able to acquire great fortunes and wealth. So take this rulebook and use it as a playbook for yourself. You might find some things you don't like. I once heard a wise person say learn to eat the meat of things and spit out the bones. So enjoy this rulebook and take whatever meat away that you can!

This book is dedicated to the life and family of Marcus Perry and Aliyah Phillips, two brilliant young people whose lives were cut too short.

I want to share the message of hope and an amazing future available for all of you who will read this book.

# CONTENTS

# RULE #1
## Love Life

I wake up early every single day thankful for another 24 hours to live.

I drink in the day.

I listen to the birds chirp.

I breathe in the fresh air or stare at the clouds with a smile.

It was not always like this. There was a time I woke up late, dragging out of bed hating life. There was a time I was depressed and broken down with thoughts of doing evil things to myself. There were so many negatives, lies, and labels I believed about myself. I was carrying a false identity that I needed to shed.

I once felt like life was not worth living and that I was an accident. I felt this way until I had a light bulb moment that made me thankful for the life I lived. I had someone speak to me and tell me that I had worth and value. That person told me they believed in me. I began to then to go through the process of learning to appreciate my life. I learned to get in the driver's seat and stop living in my past. Instead, I chose to determine my own today and my future. Today, I am passionate to let you know the truth about yourself too.

- ○ You are not an accident.

- ○ You are not a mistake.

- ○ You are not just another meaningless face in the crowd.

- ○ You are handsome.

- ○ You are beautiful.

- ○ You are brilliant.

- ○ You matter.

- ○ You are not alone.

Don't ever believe the voices that tell you life is not worth living. You have worth. You are priceless.

If you feel like you are all alone, talk to someone. Do not ever think about taking your own life. Whatever you are facing, there is an answer for it.

Do not believe the lie that no one cares about you and you are no good.

You are the solution to someone's problem. You are the answer to someone's prayer.

Someone needs your gifts, talents and unique abilities as well as your smile.

# QUESTIONS TO CONSIDER:

- On most days that you wake up, what is the dominant thought and emotion that you feel?

- List 2 people you can call right now if you are depressed or in pain that you know can help you: 1)_____
  2) _____

- If you cannot list anyone I need you to find two people immediately you can contact for support.

# RULE #2
# Make a plan for your life

A mentor of mine, Coach Al Hollingsworth taught me there are three reasons why people are defeated in life:

1. No plan

2. No commitment to the plan

3. Moving too slowly

Without a vision and plan for your life you will go anywhere and do anything and that is a dangerous place to be. Who do you want to become in life? What are your expectations for yourself? What type of student do you want to be? How do you want to be known and remembered as?

Write a vision out and make it easy to understand so that you can execute it. For example if you are a D-student, make the goal to get all C's. Find out from your teachers how you can raise your grades step by step. Remember, little by little anything is easy to accomplish.

Do you have a plan for your school year?

Set goals for your education. What is your learning goal for this year? Learning goals are based around learning skills, concepts or or attempting mastery an area of learning. Do you have a learning goal for each of your classes?

Do you have a plan for your life? Create a plan and more importantly, take action on that plan. Who are you becoming? What profession, career industry are you headed towards? What type of How many people do you know who talk a good game about all the things they are going to do? Then later on you find out that same person who did all the "talking" about doing something, in fact ended up doing nothing. You do not want to be the person that is just a good talker. You want to be a person of action.

Good, hard work brings profit, while just talking leads to being broke. In other words, don't just talk about it be about it. Your plan needs someone to put some legs to it.

Write your plan. Once you have written out a plan, go and find a person to hold you accountable to make sure the plan is put into action.

My friend Richard is my weekly accountability friend. He is the person I check in with and he checks to see if I accomplished the goals I stated I would finish in the previous week. Without having someone in my life to push me, it would be easy to back out of completing my plan. You need a person (I suggest a parent or mentor or someone you know is reliable) to hold your feet to the fire so that you get to work on your plan.

## THINGS TO ALWAYS REMEMBER:

Goals are dreams with deadlines. Turn your dreams into goals. Waiting too long to act out your plan can cause you to miss out on opportunities. Act out your plan quickly and you will be pleased with the results.

In college when I chose to get serious and stop failing classes I made a plan to sit up in front of the class daily and take notes. I also made the plan to stop cheating. You see, throughout my schooling, I learned the bad habit of cheating and thought I was getting over. All the while I was really cheating myself by not acquiring the information that I would need for life. So I decided to take the full on consequence for either my study or lack of study that I did in each college course I took. Once I took action on those plans I saw things turn around for me and I was able to see major improvement.

Make a plan for your life.

## QUESTIONS TO CONSIDER:

• What is your educational plan for this year?

• Write out one learning goal for each class you are in: Answer this question (What do I want to really learn well in this class? Example in math you might want to master your exponents, In Spanish you might want to learn how to order a meal at a restaurant or a 5 minute conversation with someone that speaks the language natively etc).

# RULE #3
# Choose your friends very carefully

Your friends are a representation of who you are. Your friends indicate the direction you are going in your life.

Friends are always to be chosen. If that last sentence sounds weird, read it again out loud. Most people you know haphazardly become friends with people instead of strategically choosing their friends. So many people make the horrible mistake of just "becoming" friends with someone. What I mean is that they don't really put much thought into the people they hang around or with. You need to be selfish in choosing to whom you give your trust and time.

## *LEARN THE DIFFERENCE BETWEEN FEAR-SHIP VS. FRIENDSHIP*

A majority of youth today (heck, even ADULTS) do not understand the difference between Friendship vs. Fear-ship

**Friendship:** The act or state of engaging in a mutual and enjoyable relationship known as being friends.

**Fear-ship:** The act of being trapped in a place of fear that you will be rejected and an "outcast" if you don't do what the person or so-called "clique" is doing.

## QUESTIONS TO CONSIDER:

- What category do you find yourself in – friendship or fear-ship?

- Are the people that you surround yourself with encouraging you to become the best you can be?

- Where are the people that surround you going with their life?

- Do you have the same values and goals as the people around you?

- Are your "friends" developing healthy habits or deadly habits?

- Are you being inspired by the people around you?

- Do you feel as if you can be your true self and not be judged when around your "friends"?

# A FEW THINGS TO REMEMBER:

If you feel that you have to put on a mask so that you won't be rejected, then you are **not** surrounded by real friends. Friends will always help you to make the healthy decision in any situations. Friends care about your best interest and not theirs — even if they will lose out. A friend is happy to see you succeed and accomplish great things. Jealousy should not exist in true friendships.

Having bullies or friends that criticize you, make you feel small, and call you all kind of names is not only a bad choice, it is extremely fruit-less. Remember, your time is valuable. You don't have time to be in a friendship with someone who is not helping you reach your full poten-tial. Instead, those type of people only drain your energy and cause you to hide behind masks. Those are toxic relationships. Eliminate them from your life.

Evaluate whom you give the title of friend to? Do they deserve the title?

Cut off the toxic friends if you don't you will find yourself in toxic situations.

# RULE #4
# Learn to appreciate your family

id you know that you were placed within your family for a reason? Yes that crazy bunch of people who sometimes drive you crazy still serve a purpose in your life. Do not curse the ground from which you come from. To speak ill of your family — wishing death, hurt and destruction upon your family is not cool. We all have challenging individuals in our family. When you really think about it, who *doesn't* have a family with some type of dysfunction? Even the family that looks totally perfect on the outside has flaws. You are not alone if you think your family is "messed up."

Some of you may not even know what the concept of "family" means. Please realize this: your family is the vehicle through which you arrived here. There is always something to be learned from your family unit. Learn to value your parents, parent, or guardian. Focus on the good in them despite all their flaws*. It may be a challenge for you to respect your parents. Your father and mother may have made some decisions that you don't agree with, but learn to respect and honor them.

---

* This does not include abusive situations. In no way is abuse whether physical or sexual ever okay. If you are in a dangerous situation, go and TALK to someone you trust immediately. GET HELP.

Personally, I grew up as the middle child and at times felt neglected and ignored. I often struggled in my family to feel like I even mattered to my family. As a child I was jealous and said hurtful things to my siblings because I wanted to gain attention. I acted out at school to get attention. I wasted valuable time hurting my family instead of building up my family. It was only when I got older that I began to appreciate my siblings, and my parents.

My family had tremendous challenges. We were on welfare for a period of time and had many hardships to overcome. You may feel like I did. Or maybe you feel that you got stuck in a horrible family. Allow me to encourage you. You may not see the benefit of your family, but I can guarantee there is someone in the world worse off than you. I would not trade anything for the things that I gained from learning how to work with my family. I love my Father and Mother greatly. I love my sister and my brother very much.

## QUESTIONS TO CONSIDER:

- Do you genuinely love your family?

- Write out 2 things that you appreciate about each one of your family members? Dig as deep as you can find these things that are positive about these members (begin with your parents).

- If no, Why?

## A FEW THINGS TO REMEMBER:

Your family is the training place where you will learn how to deal with outside relationships. If you were adopted or in foster care, or even if one of your parents isn't in your life, recognize that you still can learn from all that you experienced to develop a healthy respect for whoever it is that you call your family. I guarantee that as you take time to realize that your family is a gift, you will see some things move in motion for the better for your life.

# RULE #5
# Watch how you spend your time

Oone of the greatest assets we have is time. Time is not replaceable. You must learn to value and appreciate your time. Learning to properly use your time will bring you great benefits. You are in school right now and this is your full-time job and responsibility. There is no reason for you to be slacking off, skipping school, or looking for ways to kill time. Prioritizing is the habit of ordering things from most important to least important.

## *ALWAYS BE ON TIME*

It is important for you to get to places on time. On time to most people means at least 5 – 10 minutes early. In the real world, arriving at the exact start time of an appointment is considered being late. Weird huh? It's important to know that American society places a high value on people that learn the skill of doing things in a timely manner. Arriving at places on time is part of learning that skill.

Practice by creating a list of things that need to get done. Start by completing the most important things (also known as priorities) and work your way down. Every day, try making a list of the top three things that need to be done. Get these three things done daily and watch the improvement in your productivity go up.

# QUESTIONS TO CONSIDER:

- Are you consistently late to appointments and places you are expected to be at?

- What are ways you could prepare the day before to ensure that you arrive early?

- Write out the importance of time to in 3 sentences:

  _____

  _____

  _____

  _____

- Write out todays top priorities (3 things that must get done before you go to bed.)?

- Now write out in two sentences how you will accomplish the completion of these tasks (i.e. Instead of going straight home to get on social media, video games, phone ,sleep or reality television, I am going to a study group at school for 1 hour-90 minutes)

## *A Few Things to Remember:*

Time is valuable. Learn to see time as a precious. Ever wonder why today is called "the present?" Because it is a <u>gift</u>.

# RULE #6
# Learn the definition
# of being H.A.R.D.

I f I were to ask 10 different people the definition of being hard, I would probably get 10 different answers. I would imagine that a consistent theme would be something like this:

> *"It's when you are tough; like you don't care. You know, you do you."*
> *etc*

I would like to propose to you a new definition of H.A.R.D. For us, "HARD" is this:

## *HANDLING ALL RESPONSIBILITIES DAILY*

To skip school and act like a class clown is easy. To act as a troublemaker, sell drugs and be in a gang is easy. To flirt with boys in order to get things from them is easy (and sad).

How hard is it to break the law?

How hard is it to slack off in school or in life?

How hard is it to have sex with anyone and everyone?

How hard is it to waste your time?

Man that stuff is easy. But to pursue your dream of doing something great that is going to impact your family, friends and society, that's H.A.R.D.

To become that inventor, legislator, judge, businessperson, movie director, record label owner, playwright, actor, artist, poet, or speaker is going to take work.

## *A FEW THINGS TO REMEMBER:*

A mature person has no time to try to please everyone. You cannot please everyone. It is impossible. People will talk bad about you even when you are doing well. So it is best for you to focus your energy achieving your set goals and to spend the days of your youth handling all your responsibilities daily.

## QUESTIONS TO CONSIDER:

- What do you have to give up to model success in your future?

- *Write out the type of studying, new skills or new mentors/ friendships you will need in your life to become the future successful you?

- What types of changes need to occur for you to achieve your dreams?

# RULE #7
# Work hard,
# then Play Hard

When I was a young man in Highschool I had a good mentor and friend who taught me this valuable rule. Leisure and recreation are two vital practices needed by every single person on this planet. But let playtime be a reward for a job well done.

If you know that you have a quiz, an exam, a project or an assignment coming up, then make time to get it done. Remember, there is no such thing as "good luck." I believe that each person can create opportunities based upon how good their work is in any given situation.

Good work demands respect. People notice good work. It speaks loudly. Notice how good you feel when you take your time to make sure something is done with excellence. When you work hard you have earned the right to play hard. Go hang out with friends, go to a game, get online or play your favorite video game (guys we can get pretty addicted so watch the time), or go shopping. You feel better about yourself and less stressed out when you know the important things are taken care of.

No one likes being stressed out. When you know you have unfinished work, it can stress you out.

## SOME QUESTIONS TO CONSIDER:

- What type of person do you want to be when you are older?

- Someone who is stressed out about money, stuck in a dead end job and hating your life everyday?

- Or would you rather be that carefree person you see when you have a day off or get out of school early? You know, the one who is riding in their boat, playing in the sun and seeming like they don't have a care in the world. I think we both know that the second choice is where we would rather be. If you work hard now, you earn the right to play hard later.

- On a scale of 1-10 10 being the highest/best 1 being the lowest/worst how hard would you say you daily work toward flourishing in your current responsibilities?

# RULE #8

## You only have one chance to make a first impression. Do it in style.

Peop eople see who you are before they hear what you say. It always amazes me to talk to a young person about what type of career or vocation they intend to engage in for their future. Without fail, it is an amazing area that requires a lot of professionalism. The thing that is baffling to me is I see this same young personal covered with tattoos, an odd piercing, funny hair or their clothing is cut up, hanging off their body, or showing me stuff I never asked to see. I wonder to myself, "What employer is going to give this person a break?"

### EARN THE RIGHT TO BE HEARD

Now I know there are tons of you that can think of some idol in your head you see on TV who waltzes into corporate America with whatever type of clothing they want on their body and talks the way they want to and they seem to be respected. And you think to yourself, "I could be like that too." Well here is a little NEWSFLASH for us all: This person *earned* the right to be heard. The majority of us "regular" people out here must gain the respect of others by doing phenomenal things first. Don't make short sighted decisions that have a long term impact on your appearance. First impressions are the lasting impressions.

## QUESTIONS TO CONSIDER:

- Am I currently giving my best when I put on my clothing in the morning each day?

- Does the way I dress and carry myself speak success?

- If YES write out how you are modeling success

  _____

- If NO write out how you can begin to model success in your outward daily dress _____

# RULE #9

Great Communication
is a powerful skill worth
learning. Invest in becoming
an effective communicator.

Tow you are able to communicate will either open up many
doors for you or slam them shut in your face. Your greatest
weapons of healing or destruction are the words you use on a
daily basis. You must learn the art of using your words very carefully.
Think about what you are going to say daily moment by moment. That
is a hard task — even adults. People who speak first and think later
surround us in society. People get in so much trouble because they have
loose lips or a tongue that hurts peoples' feelings.

### JEALOUSY WORDS ARE A WASTE OF TIME

Consider are your words being wasted on foolish things like gossip,
slander, bitterness, and jealousy? One of the dumbest emotions we can
exercise against another person is jealousy. To want to be someone else

or have what they have to a point where you do not like them is immature. Learn to be comfortable in your own skin.

You are unique. You are 1 in 7 **BILLION**. You are filled with talents, skills, and abilities. You have a personality that the planet has never seen and will never see unless you exist. There is no need for you to strive to be in another person's skin. The world needs you to be you.

Profit will come when you begin to identify your point of difference? Point of difference can be defined as unique ability or attribute that makes you distinctly who you are. Some questions to ask yourself

What makes me weep?

What makes me joyful?

What activity that you engage in creates energy for you? More specifically you lose track of time when you are doing this activity?

What sort of peoples pain do I identify with? (i.e. Mother Teresa had great compassion toward impoverished orphans therefore she flourished in meeting the needs of those dear children)

Who do you desire to advocate and fight for?

These are some of the ways to identify your point of difference.

Once you understand your point of difference you will get clearer insight on your present assignment and mission in this life. You will not waste time communicating envy and jealousy toward other people. You will be too busy finding fulfillment in handling your own priorities.

Learn to rejoice when others rejoice and weep when others weep. Do it in sincerity. If you are not mature enough to practice these things, then learn to keep your mouth shut. Remember that old saying "If you can't say something nice, don't say anything at all?" It remains true.

You will find that your words will attract to you what you speak. So it is not uncommon to find a bunch of negative people hanging together complaining about things. Gossipers are friends with gossipers. Disrespectful people often swear up a storm and use foul language.

## A Few Things to Remember:

Let your words be precious and valuable. Use your tongue as an instrument of worthiness. Let the people around you look forward to hear you speak because you bring something worthwhile to the conversation.

## QUESTIONS TO CONSIDER

- Are there any people I am currently jealous of?

- Do I gossip and talk negatively about others because I am unsure of my own point of difference?

- Am I a great listener or more of a talker?

- Write out 3 ways you can use your words more effectively? 1) _____
  2) _____
  3) _____

- Who can you compliment and encourage today?

# RULE #10

## The right person is out there for you. That person will appear at the right time. Focus on achieving your goals.

As I observe the youth of today I see so many of them caught up in dead end relationships. It might be you who is wasting time on some loser who is not going anywhere or doing anything with their life. Why are there countless people that both you and I know who have drama-filled relationships that injure them for years? I believe the answer is that these people are only copying what they see. What I mean is a lot of you believe you are in school right now to find your soul mate or some love interest. You may have seen those older than you do the whole relationship tango. Television shows and movies portray high school as one big soap opera full of relationship drama. Maybe you have been mesmerized by this whole "hook up" culture of getting as many partners as you can as if it were a race.

I just want to encourage you to make healthy decisions that last a lifetime. Remember, Date Rape, Domestic Violence, Sexually Transmitted Disease, Teen pregnancy, Low self esteem, Suicide, Depression, Abuse (and a host of other things) are welcomed by having an unhealthy self worth, and unhealthy habits. People that just wanted to taste the realm of physical intimacy early have found that their experiments were costly.

There is plenty of time for you to find your mate (or have your mate find you).

## THINGS TO ALWAYS REMEMBER:

Learn to pursue your passion and develop a skill set that will last a lifetime and open up opportunities for you. I wish I had cultivated my speaking ability earlier in life instead of chasing dead end relationships. I would be much farther along in life by now. Most of the people you hang out with seem like they will be in your life forever. The reality is after you graduate, many of them you will never talk to, hang out with or even remember ever again. So invest your time in building yourself for your future.

## QUESTIONS TO CONSIDER:

- What gift, talent, skill or ability should I be becoming better at right now?

- What can I do to increase my value so that my relationships will flourish in the proper season? (i.e. are there good books on becoming a better listener, resolving conflict etc) How can you invest in preparing yourself for.

# RULE #11

# In the movie of your life, understand what part each person plays.

A reason, a season, or a lifetime

## A REASON

People are placed in your life for a particular reason. I can think back to a person who opened up a doorway for me to get me into college and they even got me scholarship money. Do I hang out with this person? Are we great friends or buddies? No. But they opened up the doorway for me to get into college based on their relationships. That relationship was to get me into that doorway.

## A SEASON

Long ago I worked with a person who gave me the opportunity to learn about my passion by giving me the chance to work with youth. That person ended up engaging in a dangerous lifestyle, made some bad decisions and is behind bars paying the price. That person served my life as a **seasonal relationship** in my development and I am grateful. I hope for them to end up making the best of their situation. But I grieved for a time and did not understand that they were only in my life for a season. This person was not in my life for me to hold onto them and get all attached.

## A LIFETIME

Then there are people who came into my life and served as key resources and wise advice. I consistently go to these people and bounce ideas off of them. I ask them for advice and can trust that they will direct me to the place that is in alignment with my life goals. These people only want to see me flourish and have served as beacons of light for me. I have been given the gift of having these few lifetime relationships.

As you grow older, you will be able to see what exactly a lifetime relationship is. I see a lifetime relationship like this: as you get older the relationships that you have with "life-timers" are not "high maintenance". Meaning more specifically time and distance (living far away from each other attending different schools etc) does not weaken your friendship. These lifetime jewel friends think the best of you and assume the best of you. People that are easily offended and want to drain your time and think you are in some sort of conspiracy theory to be their enemy are not worth keeping up the energy of that relationship.

## A FEW THINGS TO REMEMBER:

Beware of people that are leeches and time wasters. Life timers are a sure gift and rare but worthy of holding onto.

# RULE #12
## Respect Authority

Parents, Teachers, Elders, and Law Enforcement are placed in your life as a gift to protect you. You will gain authority by respecting authority.

You don't have to agree with a person or their outlook on life in order for you to respect their position. For example, your teachers who expect you give your very best effort in their classes should always be respected. For you to give your best is a reasonable expectation.

People will give you more responsibility, power, authority, and freedom based upon how you honor other peoples' authority. Because of the way that I have treated important business people, they have come to me and asked me for advice. I have been paid a very respectable amount of money to come and share my skills with them in order to bring them more profit. I do not gain business owners' respect, trust and authority by dishonoring their position of authority.

### RESPECT LAW ENFORCEMENT

When I get pulled over by a police officer, I get respect from officers because I give respect to them. I am extra careful to give them what they are looking for without an attitude even if I feel like the officer is in the wrong. There will always be immature, foolish, and power-hungry people who abuse their authority as police officers. However, it is always your response that matters. I have to do my part in making sure that I am giving out the respect I want to receive. When I am in the right the truth always comes out. The person in authority often looks silly when you respect them and don't fall into the trap of disrespect, even if they deserve it.

If you practice this rule, your own parents and teachers will begin to give you more trust and space because of it.

# RULE #13
## Don't be easily offended

Replace the idea that everyone is out to get you. You are not a victim in life. Choose to not be a victim. Life is too short to hold grudges. People who are easily offended are hard to connect with as human beings. An easily offended person is often hidden behind the walls of their offenses. Have you ever met a person who had a laundry list of all the people in their life who did them wrong? Parents, teachers, relatives, friends?

Offended people are trapped in a prison of bitterness and grudge holding. Each one of an offended person's issues are like the prison bars that they look out of everyday to see the world. Being offended takes an emotional toll on you. Have you ever been mad at someone for so long that you forgot what you were really mad about? I used to get so mad I would get headaches. It is silly to hold a grudge that long. I have seen relationships destroyed over foolish, little things.

Children are excellent examples of how we can avoid being easily offended. You can watch children play with each other, do bad things to each other and get angry. Then just a few minutes later they are back playing and acting like it never happened.

You can have an issue with a person so deeply entrenched in your heart that you carry it with you for the rest of your life. I have had people betray me. I mean *badly* betray me — like lie on me, drag my character through the mud, and still smile in my face like nothing ever happened. I've had people attempt to invade and mess up my relationship with my wife. I had to rise above being offended by these people who did wrong to me. I had to forgive them. To forgive means to release someone from a debt owed.

In order to forgive, your heart must understand that you are a person with a bunch of flaws who makes mistakes as well. Chances are you've probably offended others in the past and will continue to in the future (not intentionally). You have to recognize that other people are human just like you are. Forgiveness is not easy and takes practice.

Learn to daily think of people who have done you wrong and choose to let them go in your mind and heart. I would even go as far as saying do something nice for people who have done the most talking bad about you. It will catch them off guard.

I have purchased gifts for people who treated me like dirt. I must honestly say that it was hard to do, but giving them a gift felt really good. I actually had to laugh when picking out the gifts because it felt like something was wrong with me.

## A FEW THINGS TO REMEMBER:

Expect the best out of people and watch how things turn around for you. You can make even your enemies at peace with you if you learn the right habits. You might need to write a letter (that you might not ever send) to get your feelings out of your system or talk with an older, trusted adult. Practice letting offenses roll off your back like water rolls off a duck's back. Do not be easily offended. This will make you a champion.

# RULE #14
## Guard your gates

I n the ancient world, the gates of cities were considered to be of high importance. If the city gate could be stormed through, then the city could be easily taken over by enemies.

Each one of us has gates that serve as entryways. These gates must be protected. We have ear gates, eye gates, nose gates, a mouth gate and very important tools below our waist.

If you don't guard your gates, your state of mind can be altered to a state where you lose control. It is not in your best interest to be a person who is out of control of what is happening in your body. You might be surrounded with people in your school who pop pills, drink alcohol underage, and experiment with all kinds of drugs.

Did you know that your body is valuable? Drugs bring a false sense of peace. When a person gets high, they feel a fake sense of peace. But after coming down from the high, guess what? All their problems are still there.

## A FEW THINGS TO REMEMBER:

Drugs destroy your body. When you destroy your body you are destroying your ability to have a healthy future. There are so many adults whose families, marriages and careers have been shattered because of drug usage. You are worth more than the illusion of doing drugs. Choose life. There is so much more that I can say about this subject but you can take this principle of guarding your gates and apply it to many of the other gates I previously mentioned.

## QUESTIONS TO CONSIDER:

- Do you see your body as a temple?

- If yes, then how good of a job would you say you are doing in taking care of your temple?

- If you are currently using drugs, why are you trying to escape reality? List someone you know that is dealing with life sober and managing their lives tremendously well?

- List 4 healthy legal activities you can engage in other than drug usage? 1)_____
2) _____
3) _____
4) _____

# RULE #15
# Protect your name.
# It's all you have.

To have a good name is better than having money. A name that holds a good reputation is a name that opens doors. What is your reputation? Is it a good reputation? Or is it a bad one?

Your digital identity is the same as your real identity. You cannot afford to be caught slipping online. Did you know that the Internet stores everything? There are now many stories about young people and adults who have been denied opportunities because of a negative online persona.

## QUESTIONS TO CONSIDER

- Do your social networking activities and identity represent the type of image that you want future employers to see?

- What about the pictures you've posted online of yourself? Would they be appropriate if a college admissions board saw them? What would potential colleges that are reviewing your college application and considering admitting you think? What about your parents?

If you find yourself answering these questions with a big "NO," or are embarrassed at the thought of it, then something needs to change. If you have made mistakes, now is the time to own up and stop repeating them. Maturity is the process of growth of learning from your mistakes and not repeating them again.

## A FEW THINGS TO REMEMBER:

Clean up your name. Your name is something you will carry with you throughout your life. Don't leave a bad trail behind it.

# RULE #16
# Learn the difference between needs and wants

"**D**iscipline yields high dividends." In other words, there is a big payday for practicing discipline.

Discipline is defined as the art of learning to delay or put off your own gratification. The curse of this generation is instant gratification. People have given this generation the nicknames of "Fast Food Generation" or "Microwave Generation." The names connote a "I have to have it now" mentality.

If you learn to put off your desires and wants and focus on the things you need, you will be able to accomplish many phenomenal feats and success. There is nothing wrong with wanting nice things but is it in your best interest to waste money chasing the latest trends and fashion for the approval of people who really don't matter at the end of the day?

Do you know the difference between an asset and a liability? An asset is whatever puts money into your pocket (i.e. rental properties, certain investments, and profitable businesses). A liability is whatever takes money away from you (cars, shoes, Xboxes, games, movies, iPods, cell phones, etc). If you can learn the skill of gaining assets, you will be able to use those assets to buy the fun things that don't bring you money but enjoyment.

One of my favorite quotes on discipline:

*"We must all suffer from one of two pains:*

- *The pain of discipline*

- *Or the pain of regret*

*The difference is discipline weighs ounces*

*Regret weighs TONS"- Jim Rohn*

Anyone who has achieved great things in our society had to get a hold of this rule. Whether it is your favorite actor, singer, athlete, businessperson or politician, all of them had to use this rule to become the best.

# QUESTIONS TO CONSIDER:

- Do you personally know someone that is financially free?

- If YES Have you spent time asking them how they discipline their life?

- If NO who can you contact this month that is successful in finances that can answer some questions for you as to how they became financially free (no debt)?

- Date you will contact _____

- Way you will contact: Phone _____ ?
  Email _____ ?
  Text _____ ?
  Mailed Letter _____ ?

- Date you will follow up on your initial contact_____ ?

- Questions you will ask them:

  a) *What do you consider the most important thing I must know about money* _____ ?

  b) What disciplines have you put in your life in the past that have helped you today?

  c) What books can I read or trainings can I attend to get a better grasp on discipline?

# RULE #17
# Learn to respect and manage your money

How do you view money? Money is to be looked at as a seed. Let's take a look at an apple seed, for example. An apple seed is amazing because each seed possesses the ability to produce an innumerable amount of apples. We cannot possibly know the amount of apples that one seed will end up producing. In the same manner, see your money as a seed that cannot be wasted or thrown away. If you have a desire to be financially free then you must grab a hold of this principle.

Look around and look at these horrible businesses that allow you to borrow money on a paycheck that you have not yet received ("Cash Today" or "Cash Right Now"). Remember, the borrower becomes a slave to the lender. Owe no one. Learn to be a master of your money.

Good advice for any young aspiring entrepreneur given by Jim Rohn is to learn to _**never spend more than 70 cents**_ of every dollar you earn or are given. Here is the breakdown of what you are to do with the remaining 30 cents:

## BECOME A GIVER

A good starting point is to take 10 cents of every dollar and give it away to a noble cause. Giving away money is a great practice because it humbles you to recognize that you are blessed and there are others who can benefit from your service.

## BECOME AN INVESTOR

Take 10 cents of your dollar and invest it into an asset account or as start up monies for your future small business venture.

*{Speaking on assets imagine having enough money saved up so that when you are in college you can purchase and then rent out a house to students making yourself some profits from your roommates?}*

## BECOME A SAVER

Next, take another ten cents of your dollars earned (or given to you) and put that into a savings account. Ask your parents or a trusted adult to take you to the bank to open a savings account.

If you can practice this habit of giving,investing and saving you will be able to amass a great amount of money to be able to meet your future financial needs.

## HOW TO GET THE MONEY:

Earning money is a skill that is of utmost importance. You can earn money through various ways. Doing chores at home and asking parents or family to pay is one way to earn money. You can also start up a small business based on your own talents and abilities hire other employees to work for you. Or you can learn how to bake, mow lawns, offer to program people's remote control or even write and sell your own ebook. You have unique abilities passions and hobbies and you are never too young to use those strengths. Research what people will pay for (that is legal and ethical) and then use the skills you have to make money.

Money is a subject that deserves a rulebook of its own but this is a good starting point.

## QUESTIONS TO CONSIDER:

- Do I currently have poverty habits with money or wealth habits working in my life? _____
  _____

- What are some business opportunities right in front of me? List 2 1) _____
  2) _____

- Write out a savings amount goal for yourself in the next 30days _____ ?

# RULE #18
# Make time to
# check in with YOU

E veryday is a gift and you must take time each day to look at your day's accomplishments and actions. Take time preferably twice a day — right at the beginning of your day and then at the end of your day.

Start each day with a mind of thanksgiving. Be thankful that you have another 24 hours to make an impact in the life of others. What do you want to accomplish today? Who do you want to help out? What do you want to give? How can you make this a better day than the previous one?

There are voices of evil that whisper and make insinuations to young minds around the world. Suggestions of cutting yourself and inflicting harm to your body as a release of pressure is deadly. You must not give into that lie. Your body is a temple. You need your body and destroying and harming yourself will not bring any help to the true problem you are facing. Depression worry anxiety fear etc are symptoms of deeper issues. Get help from a trusted adult even speak with friends that you know will encourage you to not harm yourself. Treat your temple as valuable.

End each day looking at yourself and having time alone with your thoughts. Make a habit of shutting off the TV, getting offline, turning off the cell phone and being alone with your thoughts.

## QUESTIONS TO CONSIDER:

- Did you offend anyone or make anyone angry with you today (that you did not have to)?

- Did someone hurt you or make you angry?

- Are you disappointed?

- Do you need to talk to someone wiser and get help are there issues that you must deal with?

- Did you have unrealistic expectations for someone that they did not meet?

Check your daily mindset so that you do not go to bed carrying grudges or storing up bitterness and anxiety. You don't want to wake up with a headache or irritated because you did not release yesterday's issues.

# RULE #19
# Learn to make quick, informed decisions

Have you ever been around a person who cannot ever make a decision? If you have, you know it can be one of the most frustrating experiences. Whether you are eating with them at a restaurant or have project to do with them at school, making a decision seems like the hardest thing for this person and it takes forever. Maybe you have been the one who fears making a decision. Not choosing to take the risk of making a decision will never get anything done.

My wife once told me that I needed to formulate a habit of opening my mail quickly and throwing away what I did not need to keep. I had a habit of letting my mail pile up. She told me that piles of mail indicated delayed decisions. I had to agree.

## DOUBLE-MINDEDNESS LEADS TO PROCRASTINATION

A person who is double minded is unreliable in all of their ways. You want to get in the daily habit making quick, informed decisions about your direction in life. If you don't know an answer, find the answer. Ask someone who you know has wisdom to get an answer and make a decision. Do not waste time when simple decisions can be made about your direction. People who have been able to become successful in life are able to make a quick, informed decision. They get good counsel and take action. To go back and forth will lead you down a road of procrastination.


## PROCRASTINATION IS THE THIEF OF TIME

Procrastination is the act of putting off for tomorrow what can easily be done today. As we all know tomorrow never comes for the procrastinator. Procrastination is the thief of time and too much analysis will lead to paralysis. Simply put: too much thinking about a small decision like what to wear or what topic to chose for your paper, will lead for you to make no decision. Learn to make quick informed decisions.

# RULE #20
## Learn to accept correction

Hearing honest words about yourself from someone you trust is a very important part of growing up.

People rarely take time to look at themselves daily and see where they need to grow. You need mentors in your life who can point out areas where you need to grow and bad attitudes that can hold you back from your goals.

## QUESTIONS TO CONSIDER

- How do you respond when someone corrects you?

- Do you always have something to say?

- Are you always defensive?

- Do you cry or get really emotional?

- Do your parents avoid telling you the truth about yourself?

If you answered yes to any of the above questions, you need to change something about yourself. Humility is the ability to see oneself through honest eyes. You want people around you to have freedom to tell you the truth.

True friends correct one another. I have friends in my life who tell me about myself – the good, bad, and the ugly. My friends are people who are honest and able to point out the ugly habits in me that need to be replaced with new habits and attitudes.

Receiving correction is a signal to people around you that you are growing more mature. Show me a person who hates correction and I will say that person is a fool.

## CORRECTION PREPARES US TO BE THE BEST

Richard Williams is the father of arguably two of the greatest tennis players to ever live — Venus and Serena. Richard made sure to place Venus and Serena on the public tennis courts when they were young. He also placed them into California tournaments where they would be challenged and when he did not see sufficient growth Richard pulled them out and personally coached them. Being that Venus and Serena were so young, it was in their best interest to listen to their Father when he gave them his coaching. Venus and Serena's father showed them the proper way to improve their game and corrected the wrong areas. If these two young women would have been headstrong or stubborn and not listened to the correction of their father and their other teachers, I do not believe they would be rated at the top of the tennis world today.

Correction from a trusted source is not meant to destroy you, but rather to help you. A person who can hear correction and look at their self (to see whether it is true or false) is the person who will go far in life.

Learn to receive honest correction.

# RULE #21
## Raise Your Standards

As I take a look back over the years, the men and women who I respect the most are the leaders, mentors, coaches or entrepreneurs who would not settle for second best in any area of their life. What I am asking you today is: Are your standards low? Take a look at your dreams for your life. Are they too small? One way to tell that my own dreams are too small is if I can accomplish them all by myself. A big dream requires big resources and other people to help you.

Dare to dream big. There is no rule that says a person can only dream "this" far and after that they are disqualified from dreaming any more.

### RELATIONSHIPS

Are your standards low in relationships? There are millions of women who are adults and will accept any guy who approaches them any kind of way.

Occasionally I turn on the television and watch a music video and see young men acting like buffoons and clowns talking to young women like they are pieces of meat. The crazy thing is, when I watch these music videos, the women in the videos are actually acting as though they like these clowns. This my friends, is a lie and an illusion. Do not be fooled by these music stars or their paid actors and models. That is not real life.

## REALITY CHECK

Here is a reality check: Young women if a boy cannot respect you enough to approach you like he has some sense, (not just in his words but how he treats you) stay as far away from that bozo as possible.

Guys or girls who pressure each other into doing things that violate your conscience are not on your side. Get rid of those foolish people. They are distractions and can hinder you from achieving your goals.

Young men, take pride in yourself. Have an attitude of honor towards young women. Be a sincere friend to girls you know. Be the guy who brings back chivalry. Treat girls the way you would respect your mother. If you do not see a girl as worthy of that type of respect, then why are you interested in her?

## DRESS FOR SUCCESS

The clothing you wear should be an indicator of a high standard for yourself. When a person dresses up it does something to their self-esteem. Ask anyone. Even the person who enjoys dressing like a scrub feels good about themselves when they freshen up a bit. Wearing a suit or dressy outfit even makes some people stand up straight and walk differently. Take one day out of the week and raise the standard. Dress up. Come to your classes and school looking like you are about to do business. Stand out from the crowd.

## PARTY WITH PURPOSE

What type of parties do you go to? When I was young I had a pretty low standard for the types of environments I would put myself in. The more I escaped dangerous situations, the more I realized I had to raise my standard.

If you know an atmosphere is going to be loose with no responsible adults there, you should not be at that party. My friends and I started to not go to house parties that had people listening to angry music, drinking alcohol and doing drugs. Those parties seemed to only attract people looking to get into trouble. Certain parties carry certain atmospheres that produce danger and sometimes death to people.

What type of sportsmanship do you have? You might be a student athlete and compete consistently with opponents who you may even dislike. Be the athlete who has excellent sportsmanship throughout and after the game.

A quote to consider:

> *"One person practicing sportsmanship is better than a hundred teaching it."*

## QUESTIONS TO CONSIDER:

• How do you carry yourself in the classroom?

• Are you the class clown who always gets the laughs from your classmates but gets in trouble from your teachers?

• Are you the follower who just does whatever the majority is doing? (i.e. if they are noisy and disrespectful, so are you, if they are acting tired so are you etc)

I say you should choose to always be the leader who chooses the **right** decision.

## RAISE THE BAR

What type of work do you turn in to your teachers? Is your work a reflection of you? Work is an honorable thing. You want your work to demonstrate that you actually care. You want your teachers to be impressed that you are a student who cares about your education and future. One of the most exciting things for me is hearing people tell me that I am a hard worker or that I did an excellent job on a project I worked on. It is refreshing to hear someone say your work equals a high standard.

## BETTER FRIENDSHIPS

Are you raising your standards for what qualifies a person to be your friend? No person should just be allowed to be your friend. Anyone you associate with should be one who has goals and a vision for their life. Any friend should demonstrate those areas that I cover in rule #3.

Hey you!? Yes the person reading this book. You don't have to accept just anything or anybody who comes your way. Raise your standard.

# RULE #22
## Don't violate your conscience

If you have ever done something wrong and then found it hard to look a person in the eye when talking about it, you have just experienced the presence of your conscience. A conscience is defined as the sense of obligation to do right or good. Your conscience is very important and not to be ignored.

Within the daily span of 24 hours you are bombarded with a ton of messages through television, Internet, radio, cell phone, billboards, classrooms, magazines and beyond telling you how to make decisions.

Whenever making a decision, check within yourself. Are you making that decision because you feel like you will be rejected by people if you don't?

Feeling a sense of wrong, hesitation, red flags or red lights blinking in your mind are indicators to slow down or change directions.

I have been to places where I should not have been, done things I should not have done and paid the price. In my youth and immaturity I was surrounded by the lie telling me that there was no consequence for the decisions I made. "Do what you feel." "No regrets". Those were my mantras.

What a bunch of crap.

When you are left with an overwhelming sense of guilt and are ashamed of something you've done, you have violated your conscience. Whenever you feel you have to hide something, it's an indicator that you might be violating your conscience.

So many people try to drown out the sound of their conscience by doing drugs, alcohol, listening to certain music (to build up a false temporary courage), and that is sad.

## A FEW THINGS TO REMEMBER:

When you are able to easily drown out your conscience, it's is a very dangerous place. Your conscience is there to help you navigate through life with justice, goodness and fairness in mind. Everyday, practice listening to your conscience. It is a mark of maturity.

# RULE #23
# Believe in the power of one

L arge crowds never accomplish anything. Movements, revolutions and reformations are always sparked by one.

It was William Wilberforce with his relentless focus and drive who pushed for human rights and crushed the horrid British Slave Trade.

It was Madame CJ Walker who rose from the cotton fields, overcame racial discrimination, created a hair care empire, employed hundreds, gave generously and became Americas first self-made female millionaire.

Mother Teresa was one who gave her life to the service of the broken, destitute, sick and orphaned children of the world and she impacted millions.

You may have made mistakes but that is the past. The mistakes that you have made are not you. Today is a new day. You are not a slave to your past. Use your influence to lead for change in your community.

You are qualified to change your family, your community, your city, state, nation, and ultimately, the world.

# RULE #24
## Watch your plate

What you eat determines what you produce. If you eat a bunch of sugary unhealthy foods, your energy level will be low. Some of you go out to eat at lunchtime and then come back to class sleepy and sluggish. A person that has eaten unhealthy foods finds it hard to concentrate and be productive. On the other hand, a person that eats healthy foods gets energy, power and strength. Some of you choose to eat fruits vegetables, light meats and you go into class focused and ready to learn.

In the same way that natural food that you eat determines what you are able to produce, I believe the same is true of mental food. If you are eating mental junk food and garbage, that is what will come out of you. For example, what is on your iPod? If you are listening to things that drain you, make you angry or weary, or cause for you to be distracted from your life's goals, is that healthy for you?

What are you watching?

Are you a reality TV junkie?

Do you spend whole days on YouTube?

I like to call television "The Great Wealth Reducer." People can waste hours upon hours watching television (I have done it), and not gain one single skill or get closer to achieving their life goals. You must choose to guard your eyes and watch what you consume. Are you watching and listening to things that make you see and treat other people as less than valuable? Some of you will not hesitate to cuss out a teacher or parent. What have you been putting inside yourself that triggers that type of response?

Television as we know it is constantly filling up with more and more worthless garbage. Exploiting as many as possible for the ratings and ad sales. Are you going to be the product of television? The product of television is a life of frustration regret and mediocrity. Don't be lumped into the masses. Stand out from the crowd and be a producer in charge of your destiny. Filter and guard what enters your mind. Kill the predatory thoughts snakes vermin that tries to consume your productivity. Treat your mind as the garden from which you grow the fruit of your life.

## THINGS TO ALWAYS REMEMBER:

Some ideas are bad ideas. All ideas have a consequence.

The type of things you feed yourself with should have the future in mind.

- O There is a poisonous mentality that our culture feeds you that is screaming, telling you:

  *"Don't think, just do!"*

  *"If it feels good do it!"*

- O Everything that feels good is not good for you.

- O The decisions you make today will determine the quality of life that you live tomorrow.

## QUESTION TO CONSIDER:

What are you eating daily? Check your plate you might
be surprised at what you find.

# RULE #25
# Be Relentless in achieving your goals

One of the most missing skill sets in our society today is the ability to move forward through obstacles. The word "relentless" is defined as unyielding, persistent, unstoppable. I chose the word "relentless" because I feel it best describes the attitude of a winner.

Are you a quitter?

Setbacks, failures and obstacles are guaranteed in life. It is my firm belief that problems are blessings disguised in work clothes. Problems are businesses waiting to be launched. If you are able to solve a problem you will reap the benefits of the reward.

Think about all the marvelous industries that are around you that solve problems. Doctors love problems because it keeps them working. Auto mechanics, engineers, and scientists feel the same way. Name an industry that does not solve problems? You cannot. All industries solve problems for others. Society rewards problem solvers. It is a worthless and futile effort to run away from obstacles. If you can press through resistance you will always grow stronger.

Are you taking the challenging classes in your school?

Or are you taking the easiest and least challenging classes that you can?

Straight "A's" in a bunch easy classes is not impressive to colleges and more importantly impressive to you. To earn slightly lower grades (that are indicative of your full effort and attention) in grueling academically rigorous classes is very commendable. Most Universities and Colleges consider the student that persevered and grew each year in classes rather than quitting at the first sign of resistance in their classes.

## REFUSE TO BE A QUITTER

I used to be a quitter. I would never finish things. I would start something and then at the first sign of resistance or challenge, I was out of there.

I would quit jobs.

I would quit classes.

I would quit relationships.

I would basically quit everything.

One day, I got the understanding that people who achieve great things are not quitters. It was at that life changing moment I decided I wanted to become a winner in life. To be a winner I would have to step up to the obstacles I'd avoided for so long.

First I started with school. I had to push past my own comfort zone to finish college (as I mentioned earlier). School did not come easily for me. I made a decision that I wanted to get a four year Bachelors Degree and I refused to quit. Mathematics was a subject I liked least. And because of the procrastination of avoiding math as much as I could, it was the last wall I had to get over. Late nights and early morning study sessions (and much sweat and prayer) allowed me to finish math successfully. I earned that Bachelors Degree and broke a ceiling that was above my family line up to that point. No one in my family had graduated from college.

I also decided to not quit jobs when there was a little bit of conflict with people. Instead I would stick the job out and many times I got promotion as well as an increase in pay.

## THINGS TO ALWAYS REMEMBER

○ Quitters never win in life.

○ Whiners never make history.

○ Complainers are social cancers to be avoided at all cost.

Teddy Roosevelt once said:

*"For better is it to dare mighty things, to win glorious triumphs, even though checkered by failure, than to take rank with those poor spirits who neither enjoy much nor suffer much because they live in the gray twilight that knows never victory nor defeat.*

*It is not the critic that counts; not the man who points out how the strong man stumbles, or where the doer of deeds could have done them better. The credit belongs to the man who is actually in the arena whose face is marred by dust and sweat and blood; who strives valiantly who errs, and comes short again and again, because there is no effort without error and shortcoming; but who does actually strive to do the deeds."*

*YOU ARE A WINNER IF YOU WILL NOT QUIT.*

Never give up on achieving your dreams. Your very future is at stake.

For Booking Information

Go to

WWW.ITSYOURFUTURETOUR.COM

Made in the USA
San Bernardino, CA
10 March 2018